CAPRIC

December 22–January 19

Image by Andrea Lauren © Simon & Schuster, Inc.

Don't be afraid.
Be focused.
Be determined.
Be hopeful.
Be empowered.

✧ Michelle Obama ✧

LET THE STARS LEAD THE WAY

Images by Andrea Lauren © Simon & Schuster, Inc., and 123RF/Volodymyr Horbovyy

Earth Signs
Taurus
Virgo
Capricorn

Aries
Taurus
Gemini
Cancer
Leo
Virgo
Libra
Scorpio
Sagittarius
Capricorn
Aquarius
Pisces

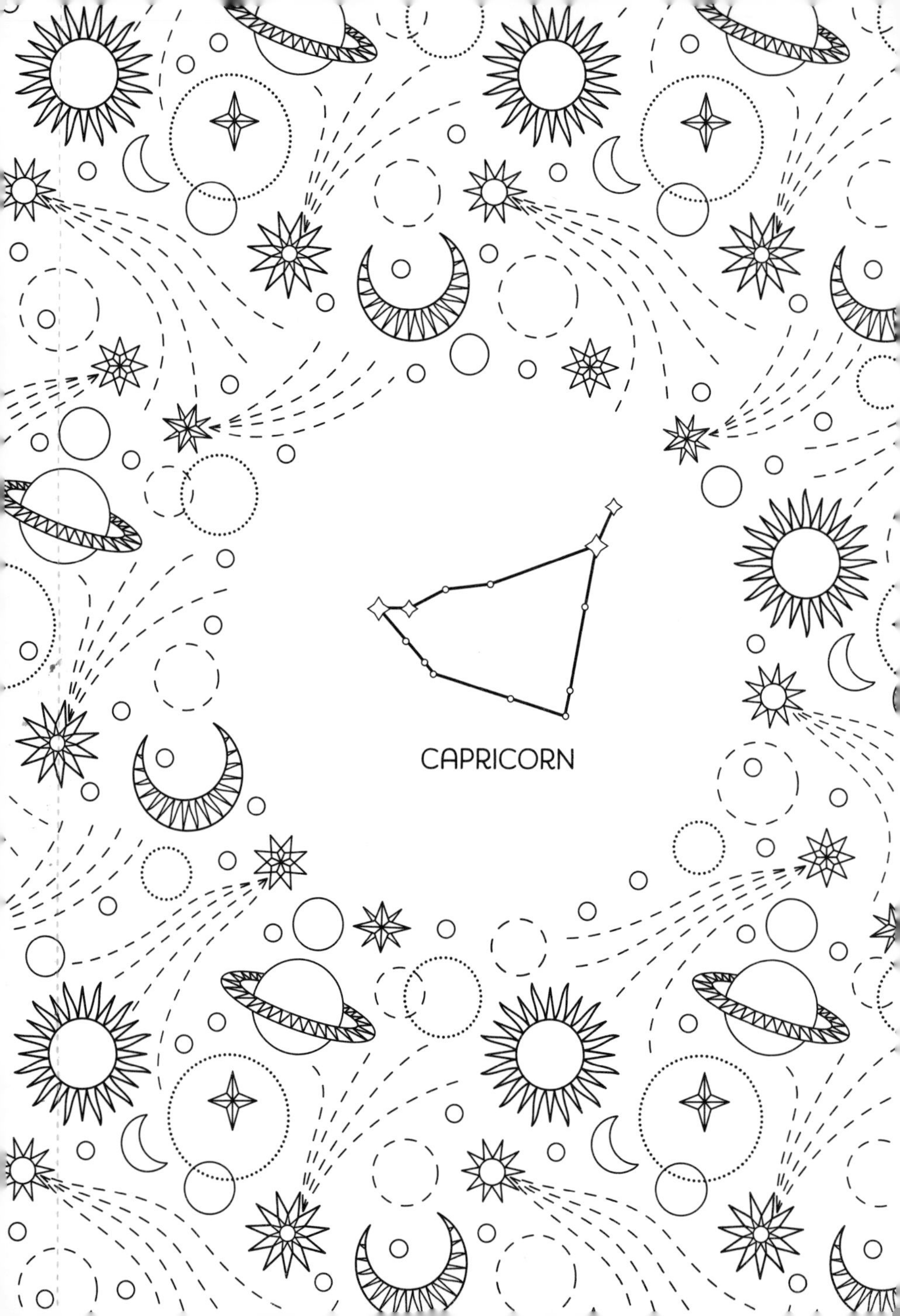
CAPRICORN

CAPRICORN

I welcome the opportunity for change

RULING
HOUSE
10
The House of
Recognition

Confident
Tenacious
CLEVER
AMBITIOUS
FOCUSED

Capricorn

Capricorn
Ruled by Saturn

Capricorn

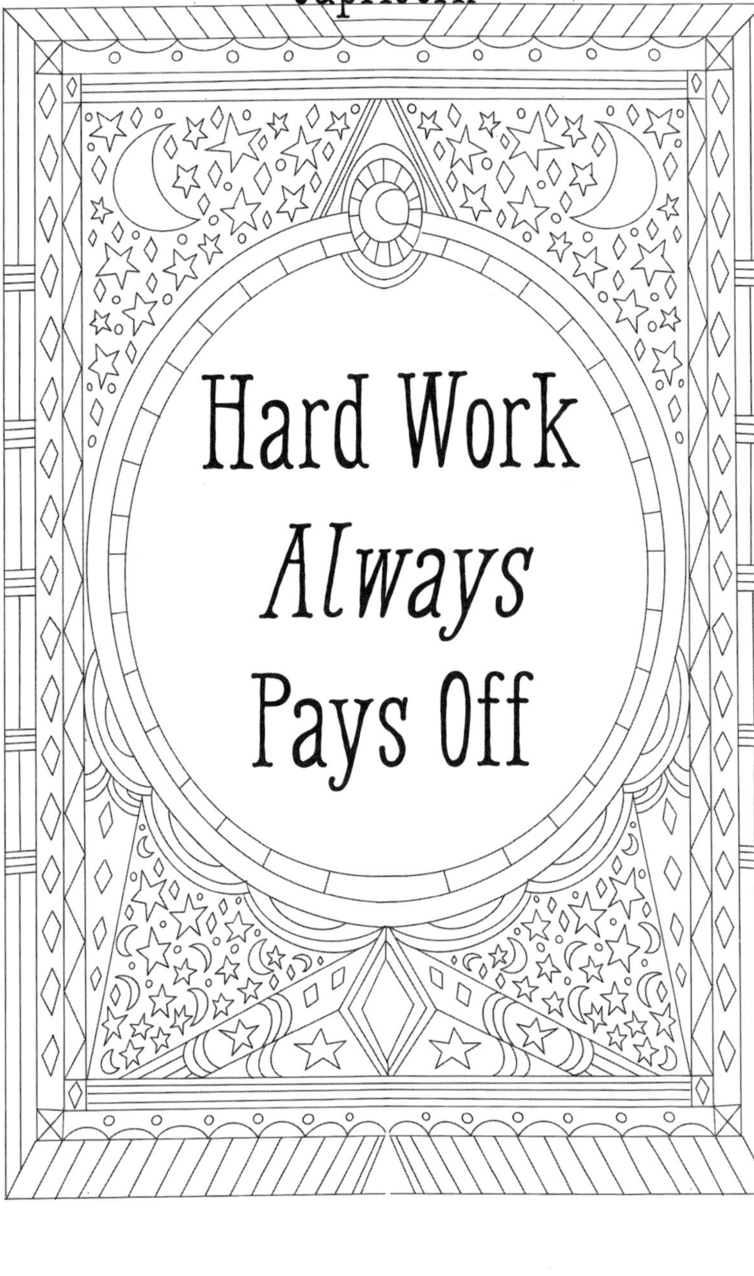

winter

Image by Andrea Lauren © Simon & Schuster, Inc.

Capricorn

I turn my mistakes into WINS